THE WORLD'S
FOOTBALL
JOKES

Jim Chumley

summersdale

THE WORLD'S FUNNIEST FOOTBALL JOKES

Summersdale Publishers Ltd
46 West Street
Chichester
West Sussex
PO19 1RP
UK

www.summersdale.com

Printed and bound in the UK by Bell & Bain Ltd, Glasgow

ISBN: 978-1-78685-209-0

Substantial discounts on bulk quantities of Summersdale books are available to corporations, professional associations and other organisations. For details contact general enquiries: telephone: +44 (0) 1243 771107 or email: enquiries@summersdale.com.

CONTENTS

IT'S A FUNNY OLD GAME

Did you hear that Sophie Ellis-Bextor
has been arrested in Paris after
someone ended up dead after a
night partying with a footballer?

**The police are saying it was
murder on Zidane's floor.**

WHY ARE SUNDERLAND FANS PLANTING
POTATOES ROUND THE STADIUM OF LIGHT?
SO THEY'LL HAVE SOMETHING TO
LIFT AT THE END OF THE SEASON.

Vinnie Jones has been sentenced to
120 hours of community service, but
this was reduced to 60 hours on
appeal – from the community.

Angus Deayton

STEVE McCLAREN IS WOKEN UP ONE MORNING BY HIS PHONE RINGING, SO RELUCTANTLY HE PICKS IT UP AND HEARS HIS VERY STRESSED GROUNDSMAN.

'BOSS! THERE'S A FIRE AT PRIDE PARK! IT'S SPREADING!'

STEVE KNOWS HIS PRIORITIES SO HE SAYS, 'SAVE THE CUPS, MAN, SAVE THE CUPS!'

'OH, IT'S OK, BOSS, THE FIRE HASN'T REACHED THE CANTEEN YET.'

'There's only one ship that's never docked at Liverpool,' explained the tour guide. 'Which is that?' asked one tourist.

'The Premiership.'

An Englishman, a Scotsman and an Irishman are wandering through the desert. They haven't eaten in days, and are hungry and hallucinating, when they come across a dead, rotting camel.

'Well,' said the Englishman, 'I support Liverpool, so I'll eat the liver.'
'I support Hearts,' said the Scotsman, 'so I will eat the heart.'
'I support Arsenal,' said the Irishman. 'But I seem to have lost my appetite.'

I met a fairy today who granted me one wish.

'I want to live forever,' I said.

'Sorry,' said the fairy, 'I'm not allowed to grant wishes like that.'

'Fine,' I said. 'Then I want to die when Liverpool win the Premier League.'

'You crafty ****!' said the fairy.

The person who said all men are created equal never stepped into a footballers' changing room.

Eric Morecambe

A supporter arrives at the ground one Saturday to find the place completely empty.

He goes to the office and asks an official, 'What time does the match start?'

'There's no match today,' replies the official.

'But there must be!' argues the fan. 'It's Saturday.'

'I'm telling you there's no match today,' repeats the official.

'But there's always a match on Saturday afternoon,' says the fan, 'even if it's only a reserves game.'

'Read my lips,' shouts the official. 'There is no M-A-T-F-C-H today!'

'Well, for your information,' the fan shouts back, 'there is no F in match.'

'That's exactly what I've been trying to tell you!' yells the official.

A man's sexual fantasy is two lesbians and a donkey making out to the music of *Match of the Day*. A woman's sexual fantasy is a man doing the hoovering now and again.

Jo Brand

Why should you never run over a Liverpool fan on a bike?

It might be your bike he's riding.

"

ALAN SHEARER IS SO DULL HE ONCE MADE THE PAPERS FOR HAVING A ONE-IN-A-BED ROMP.

Nick Hancock

BACK OF THE NET

'Which position are you playing this weekend?' asked Jim. 'Are you in goal again?'

'I think I'll be in defence, actually,' replied Bob. 'I heard the manager say I'll be the main drawback.'

Reporter: Can you take free kicks with both feet?

Striker: No one could do that – if they were kicking with both feet, what would they stand on?

ARGENTINA ARE THE SECOND BEST TEAM IN THE WORLD AND THERE'S NO HIGHER PRAISE THAN THAT.

Kevin Keegan

'WE'VE RUN OUT OF SALT AND
PEPPER IN THE CLUB RESTAURANT,'
CRIED THE HEAD CATERER.

'THIS HAPPENS EVERY MAY,'
REPLIED THE MANAGER. 'IT'S THE
END OF THE SEASONING.'

'I can't believe I didn't score that penalty,'
cursed the striker. 'I could kick myself.'

'I doubt it,' sniggered the opposition manager.

THERE'S NO WAY RYAN GIGGS IS
ANOTHER GEORGE BEST.

HE'S ANOTHER RYAN GIGGS.

Denis Law

The ageless Dennis Wise,
now in his thirties.

Martin Tyler

A match between two non-league teams took place last winter in the north of England. It had been raining heavily all week and the ground resembled a swamp.

However, the referee ruled that play was possible and tossed the coin to determine ends.

The visiting captain won the toss and, after a moment's thought, said, 'OK – we'll take the shallow end!'

WHERE DID IT ALL GO WRONG FOR US? IT WAS QUITE SIMPLE REALLY. AT THE BACK, IN MIDFIELD AND UP FRONT.

George Graham, after a 2–0 defeat for Leeds against Aston Villa in 1995

If you had to name one person to blame, it would have to be the players.

Theo Foley

A group of flies were playing football in a saucer, using a lump of sugar as a ball. One of them said, 'We'll have to do better than this, lads — we're playing in the cup tomorrow.'

ONE
ALL

WE DIDN'T UNDERESTIMATE THEM. THEY WERE JUST A LOT BETTER THAN WE THOUGHT.

Bobby Robson

For a few minutes it looked like Wigan would win, but then the game started.

Ken Ronan

THE BEST THING FOR THEM TO DO IS STAY AT NIL–NIL UNTIL THEY SCORE A GOAL.

Martin O'Neill

*The one thing I didn't expect is
the way we didn't play.*

George Graham

WE KNOW WHAT WE NEED TO DO NOW SO I THINK WE'LL EITHER WIN OR LOSE.

Ian Rush

*It's a no-win game for us, although
I suppose we can win by winning.*

Gary Doherty

WHOEVER WINS TODAY WILL WIN THE CHAMPIONSHIP NO MATTER WHO WINS.

Denis Law

WINNING DOESN'T REALLY MATTER AS LONG AS YOU WIN.

Vinnie Jones

If history repeats itself, I think we can expect the same thing again.

Terry Venables

THE SECRET OF FOOTBALL IS TO EQUALISE BEFORE THE OPPOSITION SCORES.

Danny Blanchflower

INJURY TIME

HE'S HAD TWO CRUCIATES AND A BROKEN ANKLE. THAT'S NOT EASY. EVERY PLAYER ATTACHED TO THE CLUB IS PRAYING THE BOY GETS A BREAK.

Alex Ferguson on Wes Brown

AT A LOCAL DERBY BETWEEN ARSENAL AND SPURS LAST SEASON, A SPECTATOR SUDDENLY FOUND HIMSELF IN THE THICK OF DOZENS OF FLYING BOTTLES.

'THERE'S NOTHING TO WORRY ABOUT, LAD,' SAID THE ELDERLY CHAP STANDING NEXT TO HIM. 'IT'S LIKE THE BOMBS DURING THE WAR. YOU WON'T GET HIT UNLESS THE BOTTLE'S GOT YOUR NAME ON IT.'

'THAT'S JUST WHAT I'M WORRIED ABOUT,' SAID THE FAN. 'MY NAME'S JOHNNIE WALKER.'

THEY SAY THE NEW STRIKER I'M MARKING IS FAST. MAYBE, BUT HOW FAST CAN HE LIMP?

Mick McCarthy

'Why do you always book two seats?' one Millwall fan asked another.

'One is to sit on to watch the game,' replied the other, 'and one is to throw when the riot kicks off.'

MY KNEES ARE ON THEIR LAST LEGS.

Paul McGrath

When I see a group of men walking towards me, it's always a toss-up whether they're going to ask me for my autograph or smack me in the mouth.

George Best

NORMAN HUNTER DOESN'T SO MUCH TACKLE PLAYERS AS BREAK THEM DOWN FOR RESALE AS SCRAP.

Julie Welch

The Liverpool theme song is 'You'll Never Walk Alone'. The Wimbledon one is 'You'll Never Walk Again'.

Tommy Docherty

THE GROIN'S A LITTLE SORE BUT AFTER THE SEMI-FINAL I PUT IT TO THE BACK OF MY HEAD.

Michael Hughes

JUMPERS
FOR
GOALPOSTS

As a small boy, I was torn between two ambitions: to be a footballer or to run away and join a circus. At Partick Thistle I got to do both.

Alan Hansen

'Dad,' says the striker's son, 'can you finish my maths homework while I go and play football?'
'I don't think that would be right,' replies the striker.

'I doubt it would,' says his son, 'but at least it'll look like I've tried.'

A SMALL BOY WAS CRYING HIS EYES OUT AT A FOOTBALL MATCH. SEEING HIS PLIGHT, A POLICEMAN CAME UP TO HIM AND ASKED WHAT WAS WRONG.

'I'VE LOST MY DAD,' CRIED THE BOY.

'WHAT'S HE LIKE?' ASKED THE POLICEMAN.

'BEER, FAGS AND WOMEN,' SAID THE BOY.

TWO BOYS WERE CAUGHT SCRAMBLING OVER THE TURNSTILES LAST SATURDAY AT WIGAN.

THEY WERE GIVEN A SEVERE WARNING AND DRAGGED BACK TO WATCH THE SECOND HALF.

COME ON, ENGLAND!

DURING THE WORLD CUP IN BRAZIL, THE ENGLAND TEAM VISITED AN ORPHANAGE.

'IT WAS HEARTBREAKING TO SEE THEIR SAD LITTLE FACES SO LACKING IN HOPE,' SAID EDUARDO, AGED SIX.

What's the difference between the English and a jet engine?

A jet engine eventually stops whining.

HODDLE HASN'T BEEN THE HODDLE WE KNOW, AND NEITHER HAS ROBSON.

Ron Greenwood

Oxo were going to bring out a Euro 2016 commemorative cube painted red, white and blue in honour of the England squad.

But it was a laughing stock and crumbled in the box.

Why aren't the England team
allowed to own a dog?

Because they can't hold on to a lead.

England have the best fans in
the world, and Scotland's ones
are also second to none.

Kevin Keegan

WHY DID ROY HODGSON BRING PENCILS
AND SKETCHBOOKS INTO THE DRESSING
ROOM BEFORE THE WORLD CUP GAME?

HE WAS HOPING HIS ENGLAND
TEAM WOULD DRAW THE MATCH.

*Why didn't Roy Hodgson
make it to see Santa?*

He couldn't get past Iceland.

WHAT'S THE DIFFERENCE
BETWEEN ENGLAND AND A TEA BAG?

THE TEA BAG STAYS IN THE CUP LONGER.

After losing to Iceland, the England manager thought he'd set up a friendly to try to cheer the fans up.

And if the team does manage to beat Tesco on Saturday, they'll play Asda on Wednesday.

WHICH TEAM MAKE MORE CONSIDERATE LOVERS, ENGLAND OR ITALY?

ENGLAND - WHO ELSE CAN BE ON TOP FOR NEARLY 90 MINUTES AND THEN COME SECOND?

What happens after England win the World Cup?

The manager turns off the PlayStation.

PROFESSIONAL FOUL

THERE ARE TWO WAYS OF GETTING THE BALL. ONE WAY IS FROM YOUR OWN PLAYERS, AND THAT'S THE ONLY WAY.

Terry Venables

A lot of hard work went into this defeat.

Malcolm Allison

WHEN THEY FIRST INSTALLED ALL-SEATER STADIUMS EVERYONE PREDICTED THAT THE FANS WOULDN'T STAND FOR IT.

George Best

I was both surprised and delighted to take the armband for both legs.

Gary O'Neill

SHEFFIELD UNITED COULDN'T HIT A COW'S ARSE WITH A BANJO.

Dave Bassett

One accusation you can't throw at me is that I've always done my best.

Alan Shearer

I'M NOT A BELIEVER IN LUCK, BUT I DO BELIEVE YOU NEED IT.

Alan Ball

You've got to believe you're going to win and I believe that we'll win the World Cup until the final whistle blows and we're knocked out.

Peter Shilton

WE SPOKE ABOUT IT FOR A WHILE AND OUT OF IT CAME THE FACT THAT HE WOULDN'T SPEAK ABOUT IT.

**Terry Venables, on a conversation he had –
or didn't have – with Middlesbrough chairman
Steve Gibson about his future**

NORTH OF THE BORDER

ALLY MacLEOD THINKS TACTICS ARE A NEW KIND OF PEPPERMINT.

Billy Connolly

What did the Scottish captain say to the referee when he asked if he had a coin for the toss?

'You can borrow this one, but I'll need your whistle as a deposit.'

KEVIN KEEGAN AND I HAVE 63 INTERNATIONAL CAPS BETWEEN US. HE HAS 63 OF THEM.

Craig Brown

*What's the technical term for a
Scotsman in the World Cup?*

Referee.

WHAT IS IT THAT RANGERS,
CELTIC AND A THREE-PIN PLUG
HAVE IN COMMON? THEY'RE ALL
COMPLETELY USELESS IN EUROPE.

Michael Munro

*Scotland has the only football team in
the world that does a lap of disgrace.*

Billy Connolly

For years, I thought the club's name was Partick Thistle Nil.

Billy Connolly

After last night's game between England and Scotland at Wembley, 10,000 beer cans were left in Trafalgar Square by Scottish fans. Police have arrested both of them.

It is just before the Scotland vs Brazil World Cup group game. Ronaldo goes into the Brazilian changing room to find all his teammates looking a bit glum.

'What's up?' he asks.

'Well, we're having trouble getting motivated for this game. We know it's important but it's only Scotland. They're rubbish and basically we can't be bothered.'

Ronaldo looks at them and says, 'Well, I reckon I can beat them by myself. You can go down the pub.' So off he goes to play Scotland by himself and the rest of the Brazilian team go for a pint. After a while they wonder how the game is going, so they get the landlord to put the TV on. A big cheer goes up as the screen reads 'Brazil 1 – Scotland 0 (Ronaldo, 10 minutes)'. He is beating Scotland all by himself.

A few pints later, they check the TV again.

'Result from the Stadium: Brazil 1 (Ronaldo, 10 minutes) – Scotland 1 (Angus, 89 minutes).'

They can't believe it – he has single-handedly got a draw against Scotland! They rush back to the stadium to congratulate him. They find him in the dressing room, still in his gear, sitting with his head in his hands.

He refuses to look at them. 'I've let you down, I've let you down.'

'Don't be daft – you got a draw against Scotland, all by yourself. And they only scored at the very, very end!'

'No, no, I have, I've let you down... I got sent off after twelve minutes.'

A SAFE PAIR OF HANDS

WHY DID THE GOALKEEPER HAVE SO MUCH MONEY?

HE WAS A CAREFUL SAVER.

You have to remember that a goalkeeper is a goalkeeper because he can't play football.

Ruud Gullit

WHY WAS THE KEEPER SITTING ON THE DOORMAT?

HE WAS WAITING FOR THE GOALPOST.

HE HASN'T MADE ANY SAVES YOU WOULDN'T HAVE EXPECTED HIM NOT TO MAKE.

Liam Brady

A goalkeeper had had a particularly bad season and announced that he was retiring from professional football. In a television interview, he was asked his reasons for quitting the game.

'Well, basically,' he said, 'it's a question of illness and fatigue.'

'Can you be a bit more specific?' asked the interviewer.

'Well,' said the player, 'specifically the fans are sick and tired of me.'

The Pope was a soccer goalkeeper in his youth. Even as a young man he tried to stop people from scoring.

Conan O'Brien

My computer's got the bad-goalie virus.

It can't save anything.

THAT WOULD HAVE BEEN A GOAL IF THE GOALKEEPER HADN'T SAVED IT.

Kevin Keegan

Goalkeeper: I've been asked to sign for a new team, Circus Clown FC.

Defender: As an amateur?

Goalkeeper: No, it's a fool-time job.

A GOALKEEPER THREW A PARTY AFTER HIS TEAM WON THE LEAGUE CHAMPIONSHIP. AS A SPECIAL HONOUR, HE ASKED THE MANAGER TO SAY GRACE BEFORE THEY SAT DOWN TO DINNER. FINISHING UP THE SHORT PRAYER, THE MANAGER SAID, 'AND WE THANK YOU, LORD, IN THE NAME OF THE FATHER, THE SON, AND THE GOALIE HOST.'

A GAME OF
TWO HALVES

It's the FA Cup final. Liverpool are playing Everton and the tickets sold out within minutes, with what seems like the whole city heading to Wembley. At half-time a fan, baffled by the fact that the man in front has had an empty seat next to him for the entire half when tickets have been like gold dust, asks, 'Hey, mate, how come there's nobody sitting next to you?'

The man replies, 'That was my wife's seat. We've been going to matches together for almost twenty years now, but she sadly passed away recently.'

'That's so sad. I'm so sorry for bringing it up. But do you not have any friends or family you could have given the spare ticket to?'

'Well yes... but they're all at her funeral.'

THEY SAY FOOTBALL IS A GAME OF
TWO HALVES. NOT FOR ME IT ISN'T. I
REGULARLY DOWN EIGHT OR NINE PINTS.

Adrian Bond

'Man offers marriage to woman with
FA Cup final tickets. Please send good
colour photograph of tickets.'

Advert in classified section of newspaper

ASHLEY COLE GOES INTO A BAR AND SAYS,
'JUST A HALF FOR ME, THEN I'LL BE OFF.'

A FIRST DIVISION PLAYER NOT NOTED FOR HIS MODESTY WAS REGALING HIS FRIENDS IN THE LOCAL PUB.

'I CAME OUT OF THE GROUND AFTER THE MATCH LAST SATURDAY AND THERE WERE LITERALLY HUNDREDS OF FANS OUTSIDE WAVING AUTOGRAPH BOOKS AT ME!'

NOTICING THE SCEPTICAL LOOKS ON THE FACES OF HIS LISTENERS, HE ADDED, 'IT'S TRUE! IF YOU DON'T BELIEVE ME, ASK RYAN GIGGS – HE WAS STANDING RIGHT NEXT TO ME.'

LIGHT-BULB
MOMENTS

HOW MANY EVERTONIANS DOES IT TAKE TO CHANGE A LIGHT BULB?

AS MANY AS YOU LIKE, BUT THEY NEVER SEE THE LIGHT.

How many Grimsby fans do you need to change a light bulb?

All three of them.

HOW MANY MANCHESTER UNITED FANS DOES IT TAKE TO CHANGE A LIGHT BULB?

SEVEN. ONE TO CHANGE IT, FIVE TO MOAN ABOUT IT AND THE MANAGER TO SAY IF THE REF HAD DONE HIS JOB IN THE FIRST PLACE THE LIGHT BULB WOULD HAVE NEVER GONE OUT.

How many Manchester United fans does it take to change another light bulb?

Three. One to change the bulb, one to buy the Official Manchester United Light-Bulb-Changing Commemorative Gift Pack and one to drive the three of them back to Surrey.

How many Arsenal fans does it take to change a light bulb?

Two. One to change the bulb and one to show Arsène Wenger the video to prove it really happened.

HOW MANY SPURS
FANS DOES IT
TAKE TO CHANGE
A LIGHT BULB?

NONE – THEY'RE
QUITE HAPPY IN
THE SHADOWS.

How many Chelsea fans does it
take to change a light bulb?

**One. He holds the bulb and expects
the world to revolve around him.**

HOW MANY CHARLTON ATHLETIC FANS
DOES IT TAKE TO CHANGE A LIGHT BULB?
**NO ONE KNOWS - THEY'VE NEVER
TRIED. DARK DAYS FOR CHARLTON.**

How many Liverpool fans does it take
to change a light bulb?

**None. They just sit around talking about
how good the old one was.**

How many Aston Villa fans does it take to change a light bulb?

101 – one to change the bulb and 100 to produce a massive banner showing they do still exist.

How many footballers does it take to screw in a light bulb?

Five. One to get into position to screw it in, one to kick the legs out from under him, one to snatch the bulb and pass it to his mate who then goes and screws it in on the other side of the room, and one to roll around on the floor pretending to be injured.

THE GAFFER

YOU'RE NOT A REAL MANAGER UNTIL YOU'VE BEEN SACKED.

Malcolm Allison

'Here's the deal,' said the manager. Eighty thousand pounds a month now, one hundred thousand a month in two years.'

'Great,' replied the midfielder. 'I'll see you in two years then.'

WE ALWAYS DISCUSS EVERYTHING IN DETAIL BEFORE DECIDING THAT I'M RIGHT.

Brian Clough, on his locker-room team talks

IT'S MIDWAY THROUGH THE
FOOTBALL SEASON AND A
THIRD DIVISION TEAM ARE
DOING REALLY BADLY. THE
MANAGER DECIDES TO GET
THE TEAM TOGETHER AND GO
BACK TO ABSOLUTE BASICS.
PICKING UP A FOOTBALL, HE
SAYS, 'RIGHT, LADS, WHAT
I HAVE IN MY HANDS IS
CALLED A FOOTBALL, AND THE
OBJECT OF THE GAME IS...'

'HANG ON A MINUTE,' COMES A
SHOUT, 'YOU'RE GOING TOO FAST.'

*The easiest team for a manager
to pick is the hindsight eleven.*

Craig Brown

THE MANAGER DESCRIBED HIS NEW
SIGNING AS A WONDER PLAYER.

'WHY DO YOU CALL HIM THAT?'
ASKED A JOURNALIST.

'BECAUSE,' REPLIED THE MANAGER
SADLY, 'WHENEVER I SEE HIM PLAY
I WONDER WHY I SIGNED HIM.'

*Very few players have the
courage of my convictions.*

Brian Clough

Chelsea have just launched a new aftershave called 'The Special One' by U Go Boss.

Pat Flanagan, after José Mourinho's shock departure from Chelsea

The manager rings his striker and asks, 'Where are you?'

'I'm in my garden,' replies the striker.

'Did you know there's a match on today?' shouts the manager.

'Yes,' says the striker, 'but you said it was a home game.'

" THE SECRET OF BEING A GOOD MANAGER IS TO KEEP THE SIX PLAYERS WHO HATE YOU AWAY FROM THE FIVE WHO ARE UNDECIDED.

Jock Stein

GREAT LEADERS INSPIRE THEIR MEN TO GLORY. STEVE McCLAREN WILL BE REMEMBERED AS A WALLY WITH A BROLLY.

Daily Mail

Chairman: That was a pretty dismal game today.

Manager: Well, the crowd were behind me all the way.

Chairman: Were they really?

Manager: Well, most of the way. I ducked down an alley and lost them before they could catch me.

THERE ARE TWO TYPES OF MANAGER: THOSE WHO'VE JUST BEEN SACKED AND THOSE WHO ARE JUST ABOUT TO BE.

Howard Wilkinson

Rafael Benítez was wheeling his shopping trolley across the supermarket car park when he noticed an old lady struggling with her shopping. He stopped and asked, 'Can you manage, dear?' to which the old lady replied, 'No way. You got yourself into this mess – don't ask me to sort it out!'

Even Ferguson and Wenger had their recurrent weaknesses; neither, to take a common instance, appeared capable of distinguishing a top-class goalkeeper from a cheese and tomato sandwich.

Patrick Barclay

INTERNATIONAL
RESCUE

WE LOST BECAUSE WE DIDN'T WIN.

Ronaldo

What did the referee say to the South American footballer in the World Cup who lied about handling the ball?

'I don't Bolivia.'

ONE YEAR, I PLAYED FOR 15 MONTHS.

Franz Beckenbauer

A LOCAL TEAM IN ANCIENT
GREECE WERE THREE-NIL UP
WHEN THE AWAY MANAGER
CALLED FOR A SUBSTITUTION.
THEIR STRIKER CAME OFF
THE PITCH AND ON TROTTED A
HORSE, WITH THE TORSO AND
HEAD OF A MAN, TO GASPS
FROM THE CROWD.

'OH NO, THEY'RE BOUND TO
SCORE NOW,' GROANED THE HOME
CAPTAIN. 'THEY'VE BROUGHT ON
THEIR CENTAUR FORWARD.'

I've just named the team I would like to represent Wales in the next World Cup: Brazil.

Bobby Gould, while managing the Welsh national team

APART FROM THEIR GOALS, NORWAY HAVEN'T SCORED.

Terry Venables

What do you call a Spanish footballer with no legs?

Gracias.

*The Koreans were quicker
in terms of speed.*

Mark Lawrenson

*Playing with wingers is
more effective against
European sides like Brazil
than English sides like Wales.*

Ron Greenwood

The Brazilians aren't as good as they used to be, or as they are now.

Kenny Dalglish

I'd love to play for one of those Italian teams like Barcelona.

Mark Draper

I WAS WATCHING
GERMANY AND I
GOT UP TO MAKE
A CUP OF TEA.
I BUMPED INTO
THE TELLY AND
KLINSMANN
FELL OVER.

Frank Skinner

We must have had ninety-nine per cent of the game. It was the other three per cent that cost us the match.

Ruud Gullit

FIFA STANDS FOR FORGET IRISH FOOTBALL ALTOGETHER.

Mick McCarthy

I hate it when people compare Lionel Messi with Jesus.

I mean, he's good and all, but he's no Messi.

THE
BEAUTIFUL
GAME

A couple had moved to a remote hut
in the Himalayas to escape from
the hustle and bustle of life.

'My football team lost their match
today,' said the husband sadly.

'How on earth do you know
that?' asked his wife.

'It's a Saturday.'

The last player to score a hat-trick in the
FA Cup Final was Stan Mortenson.
He even had a final named after
him, the Matthews Final.

Lawrie McMenemy

WHY ARE WEST BROM
LIKE CHEWING GUM?

THEY ALWAYS FIND
THEMSELVES STUCK
TO THE BOTTOM OF
THE TABLE.

SOUTHAMPTON HAVE BEATEN BRIGHTON
BY THREE GOALS TO ONE. THAT'S
A REPEAT OF LAST YEAR'S RESULT
WHEN SOUTHAMPTON WON 5-1.

Des Lynam

Did you hear about the new Crystal Palace bra? It has lots of support but no cups.

AN OXYMORON IS WHEN TWO
CONTRADICTORY CONCEPTS ARE
JUXTAPOSED, AS IN 'FOOTBALLING BRAIN'.

Patrick Murray

FOOTBALL AND SEX ARE UTTERLY DIFFERENT. ONE INVOLVES SENSUALITY, PASSION, EMOTION, RUSHES OF BREATHTAKING, ECSTATIC EXCITEMENT FOLLOWED BY TOE-CURLING ORGASMIC PLEASURE. THE OTHER IS SEX.

Joe O'Connor

How do you define 144 Chelsea fans?

Gross stupidity.

I'VE GOT 14 BOOKINGS THIS SEASON,
EIGHT OF WHICH WERE MY FAULT AND
SEVEN OF WHICH WERE DISPUTABLE.

Paul Gascoigne

*The problems at Wimbledon seem to
be that the club has suffered
a loss of complacency.*

Joe Kinnear

ROBERT MAXWELL'S JUST BOUGHT BRIGHTON AND HOVE ALBION. HE'S FURIOUS THAT IT'S ONLY ONE CLUB.

Tommy Docherty

John Bond has blackened my name with his insinuations about the private lives of football managers. Both my wives are upset.

Malcolm Allison

WHY DO PEOPLE TAKE AN INSTANT DISLIKE TO ARSENAL?
IT SAVES TIME.

EARLY
BATH

WHAT'S THE DIFFERENCE BETWEEN
THE INVISIBLE MAN AND FULHAM?

YOU'RE MORE LIKELY TO SEE THE
INVISIBLE MAN AT A CUP FINAL.

When you've been given a free transfer
by Rochdale you worry seriously
about your future.

Terry Dolan

WHY DID THE FOOTBALL CLUB CHANGE ITS
NAME TO 'YOU CAN'T PLAY FOR SHIT FC'?

SO IT SOUNDED LIKE THEIR FANS
WERE CHEERING THEM ON.

A QPR fan walks into a pub with his dog just as the football scores come on the TV. The announcer says that QPR have lost 3−0 and the dog immediately rolls over on its back, sticks its paws in the air and plays dead. 'That's amazing,' says the barman, 'what does he do when they win?'

The QPR fan scratches his head for a bit and finally replies, 'I don't know... I've only had the dog for a year.'

We're on the crest of a slump.

Jack Charlton

'WHERE SHALL WE TAKE THE TEAM
ON HOLIDAY THIS YEAR?' ASKED
THE EVERTON CAPTAIN'S WIFE.

'LET'S GO TO BATH,' HE REPLIED.

'BATH?' ASKED HIS WIFE. 'WHY THERE?'

'THEY HAVE OPEN-TOP BUSES,' REPLIED
THE CAPTAIN. 'THE TEAM NEVER USUALLY
HAS THE OPPORTUNITY TO GO ON ONE.'

*Southampton is a very well-run football
team from Monday to Friday. It's
Saturdays we have a problem with.*

Lawrie McMenemy

A police officer stops a car being driven erratically and asks the driver to take a breath test. The driver delves into his jacket and produces a doctor's note, which reads, 'My patient is asthmatic. Under no circumstances should he be asked to blow into anything.'

'OK,' says the cop. 'I'll give you a blood test instead.'

The driver delves into his jacket and produces another doctor's note: 'My patient is a haemophiliac so please don't ask him to provide blood.'

'Right,' says the cop, 'it'll have to be a urine sample.'

The driver produces a third doctor's letter: 'My patient is a Rotherham United fan. Please do not take the piss out of him.'

HALF-TIME
HOWLERS

WHY DID THE FOOTBALLER TAKE A PIECE OF ROPE ONTO THE PITCH?

HE WAS THE SKIPPER.

Who was the worst player in the insect football tournament?

The fumble bee.

WHY DID CINDERELLA GET KICKED OFF THE FOOTBALL TEAM?

BECAUSE SHE KEPT RUNNING AWAY FROM THE BALL.

What happened when the pitch was flooded during a World Cup match?

The managers sent on their subs.

WHY DON'T GRASSHOPPERS GO TO MANY FOOTBALL MATCHES?

THEY PREFER CRICKET.

What do spacemen play football on?

Astroturf.

WHY DID THE FOOTBALL PITCH END UP LIKE A TRIANGLE?
BECAUSE SOMEBODY TOOK A CORNER.

Which side has the shyest players?

The reserve-d team.

WHAT LIGHTS UP A FOOTBALL PITCH AT NIGHT?
A FOOTBALL MATCH.

WHY IS IT A BAD IDEA TO PLAY FOOTBALL IN THE JUNGLE?

THERE ARE TOO MANY CHEETAHS.

Why did the footballer buy acne cream?

Because of his penalty spots.

WHAT DO YOU CALL A GIRL STANDING BETWEEN TWO GOALPOSTS?
ANNETTE.

Why didn't the fans like the new stadium on the moon?

There was no atmosphere.

WHY DID THE MONK TAKE UP FOOTBALL?
HE WANTED TO KICK THE HABIT.

Which cartoon character supports Celtic?

**Yogi Bear – he always manages
to outsmart the rangers.**

WHAT'S THE DIFFERENCE BETWEEN
ACCRINGTON STANLEY AND A PENCIL?
THE PENCIL HAS ONE POINT.

What's the difference between
West Ham and an albatross?

An albatross has got two decent wings.

HOW DID THE PITCH GET ALL WET?
THE PLAYERS DRIBBLED ALL OVER IT.

What tea do footballers drink?

PenalTea.

HOW DO PLAYERS STAY
COOL DURING A GAME?
THEY STAND NEAR THE FANS.

RED CARD

Striker: Could you send me off if I said you were the worst referee I've ever known and my two-year-old could do a better job than you?

Referee: Yes, I most certainly could.

Striker: What if I just thought it but didn't say it?

Referee: Well, I couldn't do anything about that.

Striker: I'll just leave it at that, then.

IF THE FOURTH OFFICIAL HAD DONE HIS JOB IT WOULDN'T HAVE HAPPENED, BUT I DON'T WANT TO BLAME ANYONE.

John Aldridge

A man goes to heaven and tries to justify his passage through the pearly gates by telling St Peter how brave he has been. St Peter asks him for more details.

'Well,' says the man, 'I was refereeing this important match between Liverpool and Everton at Anfield. The score was nil–nil and there was only one more minute of play to go in the second half when I awarded a penalty against Liverpool at the Kop end.'

'OK,' admits St Peter, 'I agree that was a real act of bravery. Can you perhaps tell me when this took place?'

'Certainly,' the man replied, 'about three minutes ago.'

A football hooligan appeared in court charged with disorderly conduct and assault. The arresting officer stated that the accused had thrown something into the river.

Judge: What exactly did the accused throw?

Officer: Stones, sir.

Judge: Well, that's hardly an offence, is it?

Officer: It was in this case, sir. Stones was the referee.

'You can shove that red card where the sun doesn't shine!' screamed the defender at the referee.

'Too late,' replied the referee. 'It's already full of three yellow cards and a corner flag.'

HOURS AFTER THE END OF THE WORLD, A BORDER DISPUTE EMERGED BETWEEN HEAVEN AND HELL. GOD INVITED THE DEVIL FOR TALKS TO FIND A WAY TO RESOLVE THIS DISPUTE QUICKLY. THE DEVIL PROPOSED A SOCCER GAME BETWEEN HEAVEN AND HELL.

GOD, ALWAYS FAIR, TOLD THE DEVIL, 'THE HEAT MUST BE AFFECTING YOUR BRAIN - THE GAME WOULD BE SO ONE - SIDED. DON'T YOU KNOW ALL THE " GOOD " PLAYERS GO TO HEAVEN?'

THE DEVIL, SMILING, RESPONDED, 'YEAH, BUT WE'VE GOT ALL THE REFS.'

'I need a hobby,' sighed Tom.

'You should join the local football team,' suggested Brian.

'But I don't know anything at all about football,' protested Tom.

'Don't worry,' replied Brian, 'you could referee for them instead.'

I'M TRYING TO BE CAREFUL WHAT I SAY, BUT THE REFEREE WAS USELESS.

David Jones

Did you hear about the England international who had a date with a referee's daughter?

She penalised him three times for handling, interference and trying to pull off a jersey.

AT THE END OF THE DAY

A man goes into a pub with an alligator under his arm.

'Do you serve Man City fans here?' he asks.

'Certainly, sir, no problem at all,' replies the barman, nervously staring at the alligator.

'OK,' says the man, 'a pint of lager for me and a City fan for the alligator.'

A footballer lent his pencil tin to a friend, who was rooting through it and pulling out protractors and set squares.

'What's this?' asked the friend, holding up a very complex-looking piece of equipment with lots of angles and lines.

'That's an offside rule,' replied the footballer.

THE SEVEN DWARVES WERE DRIVING TO THE BURNLEY MATCH WHEN THEY SUDDENLY LOST CONTROL AND SWERVED DOWN A BANK. THE CAR ROLLED DOWN AND CAME TO A STOP UPSIDE DOWN, SO WHEN THE PARAMEDICS ARRIVED THEY FEARED THE WORST.

'HOW MANY OF YOU ARE THERE?' THEY SHOUTED INTO THE WRECKAGE.

'SEVEN,' CAME BACK THE REPLY. 'WE WERE OFF TO THE BURNLEY GAME. THEY'RE GOING TO WIN THE CUP TODAY.'

'WELL, THANK GOODNESS FOR THAT,' SAID ONE PARAMEDIC. 'AT LEAST DOPEY'S OK.'

Who should be there at the far post but yours truly, Alan Shearer.

Colin Hendry

A man took his son to see Stoke City play. He gave the man at the ticket desk £40 and said, 'Two, please.'

'Certainly, sir,' replied the ticket seller. 'Would you prefer midfieldersor defenders?'

COMMENTARY BOX

THEY'VE WON 66 GAMES, AND SCORED IN ALL OF THEM.

Brian Moore, commentating on Norwegian side Rosenborg

He had an eternity to play that ball but he took too long over it.

Martin Tyler

THIS WILL BE THEIR NINETEENTH CONSECUTIVE GAME WITHOUT A WIN UNLESS THEY CAN GET AN EQUALISER.

Alan Green

WE'RE NOW GOING TO WEMBLEY FOR LIVE SECOND-HALF COMMENTARY ON THE ENGLAND – SCOTLAND GAME, EXCEPT THAT IT'S AT HAMPDEN PARK.

Eamonn Andrews

*You can't take your eye off this game
without seeing something happen!*

Harry Gration

IT WAS A MATCH THAT COULD HAVE GONE EITHER WAY AND VERY NEARLY DID.

Jim Sherwin

*It was one of those goals
that's invariably a goal.*

Denis Law

BOBBY ROBSON'S NATURAL EXPRESSION IS THAT OF A MAN WHO FEARS HE MIGHT HAVE LEFT THE GAS ON.

David Lacey

The score is Ipswich nil and Liverpool two. If it stays that way, you've got to fancy Liverpool to win.

Peter Jones

FOR THOSE OF YOU WATCHING IN BLACK AND WHITE, SPURS ARE IN THE ALL-YELLOW STRIP.

John Motson

The match will be shown on *Match of the Day* this evening. If you don't want to know the result, look away now as we show you Tony Adams lifting the trophy for Arsenal.

Steve Rider

All strikers go through what they call a glut when they don't score goals.

Mark Lawrenson

THERE'S ONLY ONE DAVID BECKHAM

The Man United players are in the
dressing room just before the
game, when Roy Keane walks in.

'Boss,' he says, 'there's a problem. I'm not
playing unless I get a cortisone injection.'

'Hey,' says Becks. 'If he's having
a new car, so am I.'

WELL, I CAN PLAY IN THE CENTRE, ON THE RIGHT, AND OCCASIONALLY ON THE LEFT-HAND SIDE.

David Beckham, when asked if it would be fair to
describe him as a volatile player

Sir Alex Ferguson is the best manager
I've had at this level. Well, he's the
only manager I've had at this level.

David Beckham

I've read David's autobiography from cover to cover. It's got some nice pictures.

Victoria Beckham

David Beckham goes shopping, and sees something interesting in the kitchen department at John Lewis.

'What's that?' he asks the assistant.

'A Thermos flask.'

'What does it do?' asks Becks.

The assistant explains that it keeps hot things hot and cold things cold. Beckham is impressed. He buys one and takes it along to his next training session.

'Here, boys, look at this,' he says proudly. 'It's a Thermos flask.'

'What does it do?' his teammates ask.

'It keeps hot things hot and cold things cold,' says Becks.

'And what have you got in it?' asks Paul Scholes.

'Two cups of coffee and a choc ice,' replies David.

Becks needs to increase his level of fitness if he is to impress at Real Madrid, so he goes to see a Spanish doctor.

'What I would advise you to do,' says the doctor, 'is run five miles a day for the next fifty days and then come back and see me.'

Fifty days later, the doctor receives a phone call from Beckham.

'I thought I told you to come back and see me,' he says.

'I can't,' replies David. 'I'm two hundred and fifty miles from home and I don't know the way back.'

David Beckham has snubbed a move to Paris Saint-Germain: 'German is a hard language to learn and I want to finish trying to learn American.'

SICK AS A
PARROT

MY GIRLFRIEND JUST SPLIT UP
WITH ME BECAUSE SHE THINKS THAT
I'M OBSESSED WITH FOOTBALL.

I'M A BIT GUTTED. WE'D BEEN GOING
OUT FOR ALMOST FOUR SEASONS.

What is the difference between
Coventry and the Bermuda Triangle?

The Bermuda Triangle has three points.

WHAT'S THE DIFFERENCE BETWEEN A
LIVERPOOL FAN AND A BROKEN CLOCK?

EVEN A BROKEN CLOCK IS
RIGHT TWICE A DAY.

'I'VE JUST BOUGHT A TOTTENHAM ROVING SEASON TICKET,' BOASTED ROBERT.

'WELL,' REPLIED GARY, 'I'VE JUST BOUGHT AN INTERRAIL PASS. THAT'S MUCH BETTER.'

'WHY'S THAT?' ASKED ROBERT. 'YOU WON'T SEE MUCH FOOTBALL WITH THAT.'

'MAYBE NOT,' GLOATED GARY, 'BUT AT LEAST I'LL SPEND LONGER THAN NINETY MINUTES IN EUROPE.'

What's the difference between
Alex Ferguson and God?

God doesn't think he's Alex Ferguson.

I DON'T THINK WE'LL GO DOWN. BUT THEN AGAIN, THE CAPTAIN OF THE *TITANIC* SAID THE SAME THING.

Neville Southall, on Everton's chances of
avoiding relegation

Man United have set up a call centre for
fans who are troubled by their current
form. The number is 0800 10 10 10. Calls
are charged at peak rate for overseas
users. And once again, the number is 0800
won nothing won nothing won nothing.

If you're interested in finding out more about our books, find us on Facebook at **Summersdale Publishers** and follow us on Twitter at **@Summersdale**.

www.summersdale.com